Hearing Voices

ALSO BY ERIC COATES

*Cracking Up: A Memoir of Love, Drinking,
Drugs, Poverty, Paranoia, and Other Afflictions
on the Road to Madness*

Hearing Voices

· A MEMOIR OF MADNESS ·

Eric Coates

What is there in any human being's experience to prepare him or her to cope with a broken brain? Who can understand what a catastrophe this break is for the human soul?

— Dr. Jane Doller, from *The Quiet Room* by Lori Schiller and Amanda Bennett

1.

Schizoaffective illness, for anyone who wants to know, is defined by the authorities at the Better Health Channel (www.betterhealth.vic.gov.au) as a 'combination of two mental illnesses — schizophrenia and a mood disorder,' a pretty unremarkable definition, whose two types of 'associated mood disorder' are 'bipolar (characterised by manic episodes or an alternation of manic and depressive episodes) and unipolar (characterised by depressive episodes).' According to this definition, there are 'two subtypes,' the 'schizoaffective bipolar type' and the 'schizoaffective depressive type.' Each of these subtypes has a variety of symptoms. Symptoms of the depressive type include 'loss of motivation and interest, fatigue, concentration difficulties, physical complaints such as headache or stomach ache, low self-esteem, suicidal thoughts, loss of appetite,' and 'insomnia,' while symptoms of the manic type include 'increased social, sexual and work activity, rapid thoughts and speech, exaggerated self-esteem, reduced need for sleep, risky behaviours, impulsive behaviours such as spending sprees,' and 'quick changes between mood states such as happiness to anger.' Between these two types of symptoms, or off to the side of them somewhere, there is a third group of symptoms, typical of schizophrenia, called 'psychotic symptoms.' According to *The ICD-10 Classification of Mental and Behavioral Disorders*, put out by the World Health Organization, to be schizoaffective 'at least one and preferably two typically schizophrenic symptoms . . . should be clearly present' along with either depressive or manic symptoms or both. Psychotic symptoms (again according to the Better Health Channel) include 'losing touch with reality, hallucinations, delusions, disorganised thoughts, chaotic speech and behaviour, anxiety, apathy, blank facial expression,' and 'inability to move.'

It is precisely in regards to *losing touch with reality, hallucinations, delusions, disorganised thoughts, chaotic speech and behaviour, anxiety, apathy, blank facial expression,* and *inability to move* that we are concerned here, for this is the set of symptoms, horrifying in its range, that I had myself until only a few months ago — an experience which I am only starting to sort out now. Needless to say, psychotic symptoms take a little while to recover from. In my own case it has taken me the better part of a year to get some renewed energy, for the mysterious aches and pains that riddled my consciousness and my body to disappear, and for the voices that once raged in my head to come under control. My hold on reality is growing firm again, after being shaken a long time, and I am just now overcoming an aversion to looking back on what happened to me, which was spectacular, grotesque, and like torture.

But to return to the facts. Schizoaffective illness is fundamentally 'a form of schizophrenia,' according to the Better Health Channel, or at least it is believed to be so by most 'mental health professionals,' although that is hardly the only thing about the disorder that is unclear. The cause is 'unknown,' though it is believed to be triggered by a combination of factors, including 'genetic susceptibility,' 'environmental factors such as stress,' and 'imbalances of brain chemicals.' There are a variety of treatments, which also goes to suggest that the cause of schizoaffective disorder is less than well understood; it is enough to simply review the sheer diversity of them to get the impression that we are still, somehow, in the Middle Ages. Treatments include a range of medications, electroconvulsive therapy, old-fashioned talk therapy, and a beast called 'psychosocial counseling,' which is meant to 'help the person avoid the common pitfalls of mental illness such as unemployment, poverty and loneliness.' Support from family and friends is also deemed highly important, as the schizoaffective are likely to need money, encouragement, a place to stay. They may be unable to function for several months, or several years.

Adding insult to injury, diagnosis of the disorder is difficult because of its close resemblance to both schizophrenia and the mood disorders (bipolar disorder and depression). At certain stages, a schizophrenic may display symptoms that are similar to depression or a depressive may hallucinate like a schizophrenic. Schizoaffective is a 'spectrum disorder,' meaning that a specific case lands somewhere along a possible range of symptomatology. As laid out by some professionals, this range runs from 'bipolar' (or 'depressive') to 'schizoaffective, bipolar type' (or 'schizoaffective, depressive type') to 'schizoaffective, schizophrenic type' to 'schizophrenia.' Knowing exactly which it is can be difficult, but no matter; as one doctor wrote in an on-line chat, 'fussing over whether it should be called bipolar, or called schizoaffective, bipolar type, often means very little as far as prognosis or treatment' goes, especially since the drugs — the antipsychotic drugs — used to treat them are most often the same. If this frank expression of ignorance is illuminating, consider the general attitude of the psychiatric profession. 'We only treat symptoms,' as one respected psychiatrist told me, 'not the underlying cause.' As T. M. Luhrmann put it in her book *Of Two Minds*, "Psychiatric medications treat symptoms, not diseases. They touch the way people act, not the underlying mechanisms."

None of these things, however — 'spectrum disorder' or 'depressive' or 'bipolar' subtype, or the almost bizarrely wide range of symptoms and treatments — tells you what the disorder is actually like, and the fact is that probably no one could sum it all up adequately; the cases are simply too various. Clearly, someone who is suffering from 'loss of motivation and interest, fatigue,' 'low self-esteem,' and 'suicidal thoughts,' is having a radically different experience from someone who is experiencing 'increased social, sexual and work activity, rapid thoughts and speech,' and 'exaggerated self-esteem;' just as he or she may be having a radically different experience from someone who is having 'hallucinations, delusions, disorganised thoughts,' and 'anxiety;' and when these symptoms are jumbled together the common ground may be difficult if not impossible to find. What I would like to do, however, is to tell what it has been like for me, and to try to shed some light on the subject, if only by staring as hard as I can into the darkness that has surrounded me.

2.

Among what are believed to be the basic causes of schizoaffective disorder — 'genetic susceptibility,' 'environmental factors such as stress,' and 'imbalances of brain chemicals' — it is of course impossible for me to say whether my brain chemistry is out of balance, or even to determine whether I am 'genetically susceptible' to schizoaffective disorder, since I don't know enough of my family history. (People fortunate enough to know their family history — although it is hard to imagine anything 'fortunate' about this illness — are in a better position to determine if the cause of their disorder is genetic, since schizoaffective runs in the family.) I do know, however, that stress had something to do with it; it is in fact something that my mother, the only person to closely witness both of my major breaks, has remarked on. From well before the onset of my first break, she knew something was wrong. There was a 'stressed out' sound to my voice, she calls it, bad enough to signal her mother's intuition that she should be on the watch for something.

Of course, it should be noted that my mother's intuition has been working overtime very nearly since I was born, not because I was in any way a troublemaking or difficult child as because I have always been very changeable. From the beginning I had a very bipolar personality; I was one of those people who is outgoing and upbeat and full of energy and ideas one moment, and just as likely to be feeling down, introverted, and depressed at the next. I was a classic case of the moody artist, as I fancied myself to be — a writer — and the fact is that I was someone who could be counted on to be unreliable. I had trouble handling my money — a classic bipolar symptom — but I also had the energy to pull myself out of most of the holes I got myself into. The worst thing I experienced during the downswings was an occasional case of the blues, especially acute from November to February, and the worst thing I experienced when I was upbeat was too many ideas; I couldn't keep up with them all. It is clear to me now that I always had bipolar symptoms, even if they were generally mild — that is, not the kind that disrupt a normal existence.

When I grew up, my choice of profession was calculated to give me the freedom I wanted both to dress as I liked — I had a horror of business dress with its cheap suits and gaudy ties — and to make my own hours. I started out in New York with a small publishing firm and, within a couple of years, went freelance as an editor and book designer; from then on I was able to move from job to job with a great deal of freedom. It was not the most stable way of living — there were down times between jobs or whenever I moved, and I lived in several cities — but for the most part I was happy doing what I did, which kept me involved with books, my first love. I was able to move from city to city quite easily.

I fell in love, once, when I lived in New York City (a disaster unto itself), but most of my relationships were short-term affairs until I met my former partner in San Francisco. I was out on the West Coast for a business trip when I met her and I impulsively moved there to be near her. We were together a couple of years, during which time we moved back to New York and then, a surprise to us both, found out she was pregnant. The relationship was never terribly stable, however, and after the birth of our daughter we separated; she moved with our daughter to Portland, Oregon, where she was from. It was when I tried to follow her there, wanting to be there for our daughter, that my first real break occurred.

From the beginning, my life in Portland can best be described as simply hanging on however I could. From the first minute I got there, I could not seem to hold onto a job; first one company fired me, and then another company downsized. Work was not my only trouble, however. I lived in a dangerous neighborhood, and when I had trouble paying my bills, my landlord began to harass me — by shutting off the lights, leaving threatening notes under the door — over $35 I owed him. I felt unsafe at home, and I knew almost no one; certainly no one, outside of my ex, who cared I existed.

All of this, of course, would make life difficult enough, but what made it all worse was that I was charged with a crime. On and off over the months, my ex-girlfriend and I had muddled along through a difficult relationship, ranging from periods of happily almost being together to periods of estrangement and indifference. One night, when alcohol was involved, we had an argument. I broke into her house and threatened her. The police were called and I was arrested. Since I more or less owned up to everything — thus showing my inexperience with the justice system — my conviction seemed almost certain. The possible sentences ranged from three to five years — a period that, given the reality of prison, I did not really expect to survive.

What my mother remembers is that as the date of my trial approached I became more highly strung. I would not be able to describe how I appeared to other people, which means I cannot confirm or deny what she remembers, but I do know that I tried to push the thought of prison out of my mind. What actually happened — the actual circumstances of my break — are worth a moment to describe. At the suggestion of a neighbor, I had gone to work for a telemarketing firm, the one job I could find at that time. At first I found it acceptable — at least I wasn't out in the rain as I had been, at one point literally digging ditches for a contractor — and things were going along well enough, until I noticed the shady way things were done around the company. Depending on the poor language skills of emigrants and the faulty reasoning of the aged, the company callers frequently signed people up for services they didn't really want; the person called often didn't realize they'd bought anything at all. This led to many of their sales. As far as I could tell, the company was raking it in because of this practice, and it seemed to me that everyone knew it. I made no secret of my refusal to be part of what was happening, and, further than that, I made comments about reporting the scam to the authorities. As a result I was largely ostracized. What led to my break was a moment one morning, as I walked into work, when a young man I had never seen before appeared at the line of cubes next to mine. I cannot recall the exact words he said, or that I thought he said, but I believed they were threatening, and I turned to ask him what he said. He ignored me, then and for the rest of that day. After work, I went home, and then to the bookstore, the one place I visited almost every night — or, in other words, the one place you might predictably find me — and I began to browse around. It happened to be Halloween, a fact that is relevant only because the place, normally crowded, was practically deserted; clearly, everyone was out at parties or bars. The young man, however, was there, and when I walked around a corner, almost into him, he turned away and seemed to hide his face. At that moment I became convinced — instantaneously, and without conscious thought — that he was there to hurt me.

There are two things I want to say about this.

First of all, that this first break was instantaneous in nature is something I now find to be typical. It's true that I had been building up to it for weeks, but when it happened it was instantaneous. I went from believing something perfectly normal — that the young man was *there* — to believing something delusional, that he was *there to kill me*. It was as if a light switch had been turned on in my awareness.

The second thing that I want to say is that the paranoid nature of the break is also typical. Later, after this first break was over, I could recall bouts of paranoid feeling going back through my entire life — as far back as the fourth grade. Paranoia was the symptom that most persisted after I got out of the hospital. Indeed, for a couple of years after the disposition of the crime I was charged with — that is, well after I entered a guilty plea in return for three years of probation — I sometimes experienced the sensation of being followed, particularly when I was traveling. I could not go to a strange city without feeling it. (That there actually were people who were paid to follow me, sometimes — probation officers — was an irony that went unappreciated.)

*

I had no other psychotic symptoms beyond paranoia, agitation, and a set of delusional beliefs. It was, in other words, and compared to my second break, a relatively mild occurrence. The antipsychotic Haldol was enough to bring me out of my psychosis and I was diagnosed as bipolar. When the break ended, it took me about a year to recover — that is, for all the anxiety to go away and to feel as sharp and as capable as ever.

During my first break, there is another instance of psychotic paranoia I remember clearly. This took place after I 'recognized' the young man from work (and of all the things that happened, the one thing I still feel sure of — as opposed to knowing, which is never certain — is that I *did* recognize the young man from work; after all, I experienced it as 'real' at the time, and that is how I remember it).

For a couple of days after 'recognizing' the young man, I engaged in a desperate race to hide myself. I was certain that a gang had somehow become involved — perhaps the bigwigs at the calling company had put out a 'hit' on me with some gang members one of them knew — and I was certain, wherever I went, that I was being followed. I could not go home, because that was too obvious, and I ended up taking a room in a motel. After a couple days of desperate panic and not sleeping, my anxiety level was so high that my mother was concerned for my health. I had gotten in touch with her, told her the whole story — the scam being run by the company, the young man I had seen at work and later at the bookstore — and she was convinced I needed help. The terrible part to her was that as wrought up and paranoid as I seemed, the way I talked still sounded rational. It was clear that I believed what I was saying, and it was just as clear to her that it sounded crazy, regardless of how rational I sounded. But there was nothing she could do: she lived on the east coast, I on the west coast. She thought of a way to get me into the hospital. 'Tell them you're anxious,' she said, 'and they'll admit you.' She mentioned that a psych ward had metal doors. 'You'll be safe,' she told me, and safety — it was my primary concern at that point — is what sounded good to me.

I was admitted at night, and it was only in the morning — after a good night's sleep, aided by sedation — that I discovered that the psych wing, which I had imagined to be high in some building somewhere, was actually *on the ground floor*. This thought filled me with alarm. Instead of being secreted away in a tall building somewhere, invisible to the public, as I had believed, I was being held in a ground-floor wing where all you had to do was walk around and look in the windows to see inside. Far from safe, I was actually a fish in a barrel, if someone figured out how to get inside. Naturally, I began watching the windows. I was not worried about the other patients, because all of them had been admitted before me and thus could not be part of the conspiracy or gang or whatever; there had been no way of knowing I was headed there. But I studied all of the new patients carefully, and I did not have to wait long before someone fit the bill. It was a new young man, one who was impressively built — his neck and shoulders reminded me of a bull — and I became convinced that, when he had me in a corner, he would try to hurt me. The only way he could obtain a weapon, it seemed to me, would be on his food tray, and I surprised everyone by accusing him and the janitor who brought in our food of having something concealed there. In my panic to save my life, I had made phone calls to my lawyer, asking him to send the police, which he did. (It still amazes me, but he did.) The police arrived in time to see me given a shot, for me to be heavily sedated, and to be locked in a room where the staff checked on me periodically.

3.

At the time of the second break, about five years after my first break, the circumstances of my life could not have been more opposite. Whereas before I had been down and out, living hand-to-mouth and just scraping by each week, now I was living comparatively high, running my own business and experiencing an unprecedented level of success. In fact I had just acquired the largest contract I had ever had; it seemed that things were gearing up. That I worked almost constantly did not seem too high a price to pay; it seemed to me that there was no other way to success. At the time I considered myself happy, glad to be doing my work and getting ahead. Blithely I dismissed my earlier break as a one-time occurrence, purely the result of anxiety. I gave no thought to the idea that I might again be experiencing mania.

Mania, however, was the one thing my mother homed in on. I never stopped working, it seemed to her, and she was concerned that I might either stress out or burn out. She reproached me a couple of times about it, to express her concern, but I pooh-poohed all her worries by saying things would only be like this a while. I was working, at that point, maybe fourteen hours a day, maybe twelve. When not working I was out at the bar and frequently smoking marijuana, considered by most professionals to be a trigger for schizophrenia.

The exact nature of my paranoia this time — and this is the second time paranoia has been involved — was connected not only to how much I was working but to something I was working on, and this is a story unto itself.

In January of 2005, I was working as a book designer, and I received a manuscript from a man who was a twenty-year veteran of the New York City emergency medical services, a paramedic who had been present on the morning of 9/11 and who blames the fire department for much of the disaster. According to him, the doors on the roof of the World Trade Center were locked, in order to prevent the kind of high-rise helicopter escapes that had so embarrassed the fire department during the 1993 World Trade Center bombing, when a police helicopter rescued a number of people from the roof. According to him, the FDNY is so corrupt that whistleblowers — people who point out both corruption and ineffective policies — are sent rubber rats and threatened, when not actually harmed.

According to him, the public would react when it
learned this truth and there would be scandal. The
FDNY, according to him, would do anything to hush
this truth up.

The book was a hot potato, frankly, and I wanted to get
it out of my lap. Unlike a conspiracy theory, there were
facts at the heart of this story. If true, it was a deadly
truth, and this was just the excuse that my paranoia
needed to seize on with a vengeance. I had many conversations with the author in which he expressed the
dangerousness of the book, how explosive it would be.
I believed him completely and sincerely. As I entered
into his world, his urgency had an effect on me. I trav-
eled from Portland to New York City, where I met with
him and attended a book show. During this time we
had many conspiratorial conversations over the phone.
I do not remember the exact instant it started, but I
began to fear that I might be followed; that someone
might be out to get me. I didn't know just precisely
who that was, but it had to be someone involved with
this book. It began in New York and intensified once I
had returned to Portland; and again, as in my first
break, a stranger was involved. It was late one night,
and I was walking back home from the corner store. As
it happened, I was wearing a new pair of shoes that I
had hunted down while I was in New York, something

that looked new and modern, a pair of shoes that had bright orange stripes on them. As I passed what looked like a homeless man, he turned to address me. 'Those are quite the shoes,' he said. Yes, I said, they were. And then he said what sticks in my memory. 'They'll be the last thing they see as you go over the railing,' he said. 'You know what I mean?' I nodded and continued walking home, puzzled by what he meant, but when I returned shortly after — thinking to question this stranger about what he meant — he and all his friends were gone.

At that moment — again, *instantaneously* — I believed that there was a secret war going on around me, that I was somehow being drawn into a conspiracy and that some kind of shadowy force was out there; that some secret government agency was putting its weight behind this book. There was one side (the FDNY) and there was the other (people in the government who opposed the FDNY). I was being warned to be careful. My shoes would be the last thing they saw when I went over the railing.

4.

And now it is time to introduce The Vortex.

Immediately after meeting the your-shoes-are-the-last-thing-they'll-see man I went back to my apartment and turned on my computer. After all, I was working fourteen hours a day and there were things to do. There was one email. It was labeled PCH.

PCH, I know now, was Publisher's Clearing House. At the time I paid little attention to that. I had done a singular job of avoiding spam at that point and so its mere presence in my in-box made it stand out. And once I opened it all I knew was that this email prompted me to a list — to many lists — of categories that it wanted me to respond to.

Instantly — it was the same as before — I knew that this was a special message. Nowadays the website says 'Win $10,000,000' and 'SuperPrize Winner Announced on NBC!' All I saw then was the prize and I realized — *instantly* — that here was the mechanism by which I was to be rewarded for my work. The message was

really a front — an organization set up to disguise what
they were really doing. This was their way of inducting
me into the organization.

The sheer variety of it all was enough to dazzle me.
Not only was I to win the money, but I had to sign up
for 'prizes' that ranged from children's products — I
had a five-year-old at the time — to pay-day lenders,
from skin-care products to real estate dealers who
wanted to give me unbelievable deals. The range of
these products was stupendous. It is without exaggeration that I say I merely filled in information in these
many categories from midnight til dawn. After a while
all these prizes seemed to me a kind of Vortex in which
I had been caught. Dozens of categories gave rise to
hundreds of other emails that arrived in my inbox
faster than I could respond to them. Clearly I had been
selected for a select group. I knew — I knew — that
this was how a secret government agency rewarded
those who did its work loyally. There was one level of
society — the one I had always known about and oper-
ated within — and there was another on top of it that
I was just learning about. But it was a strange form of
secrecy. There were no secret accounts, no secret pay-
checks; it was done out in the open, through these kinds
of prizes; the agency set it all up. They set you up for
life and afterwards you did whatever they needed.

The phone calls started in the morning. I have several pages of notes that I scribbled down while fielding these calls: names, numbers, type of business. The callers included debt-reduction specialists, pyramid-scheme-like business offers (most of them seeming to deal with exotic fruit extracts from places like South America or Africa), the vendors of cheap vacations and payday loans and on-line courses and job-training services — all businesses that had been prominently featured by the Vortex. It is no exaggeration to say that as soon as I was finished with one phone call, the phone would ring again.

In my mind all of these things had an explanation. Payday loans? A quick way to get cash that I would never be required to pay back — the paperwork would get lost. Debt reduction? That explained itself. Business offers? From the sound of them they were little more than free pipelines of cash; you found your place in the pyramid and it just flowed in. Job training? Well, as some sort of agent of this conspiracy, it would obviously be necessary for me to sometimes work undercover; the more skills I had, the better I could blend in. Real estate? Again, *they* were just taking care of you.

It was when a car dealership called that I got really interested. Bear in mind that I had bought a new car only the year before — new to me anyway: a Jeep Cherokee in great condition and with remarkably low miles. It filled all my needs and I liked it. But a new car? And at the low-cost financing they were offering? Why not?

At the dealership I found a car that I liked and asked about the terms. It seemed like a good deal to me. The only problem was my mother; she was an accountant and at that point, running my own business, managing my life, I found her help invaluable and left my financial affairs in her hands. If I was going to buy this car, I needed to talk to her. And the first thing she wanted to know was what was wrong with the car I had. This was an unanticipated objection but I met it smoothly and lied. There was something wrong with my car, I told her; I thought the drive train was damaged: in any case it was performing badly.

Again, my mother knew immediately that there was something wrong. It was the sound of my voice.

5.

If it has not become clear already, I would like to point out that there was something gradual about the way my delusions progressed. At first, there was simply a feeling of something wrong, something that showed in my voice in the weeks leading up to and then, with greater strength, immediately following a break. Following a break — or the moment when I can identify slipping from something that might still be called vaguely normal into something that would clearly be called psychotic — there were many stages in the progress from being merely delusional to full-blown psychosis. In the case of my second break, I did not show all my psychotic symptoms until well over a month or even two months had gone by. And a month, if you are going through what I went through, is a long time indeed.

Losing touch with reality, hallucinations, delusions, disorganised thoughts, chaotic speech and behaviour, anxiety, apathy, blank facial expression, and *inability to move.*

Not everyone displays all the same symptoms. The first symptoms I had, clearly enough, were *losing touch with reality* and *delusions*, this being the name for believing something as crazy as the idea that a shadowy conspiracy is tracking your every move. This is relevant because from the paranoid and instantaneous moment of my break, I was sure they were everywhere. Wherever I went, I was followed — or so I thought — with the result that I always kept an eye out on the person beside me, on the people behind me. *They* were following me, and the other *they* — the *they* working against my *they*, the opposite conspiracy — were out there as well.

6.

Paranoia is worth exploring.

According to the surprisingly full wordIQ.com entry at the time of this writing,

> In popular culture, the term paranoia is usually used to describe excessive concern about one's own well-being, sometimes suggesting a person holds persecutory beliefs concerning a threat to themselves or their property and is often linked to a belief in conspiracy theories.

That is how we see it nowadays, at least. But, 'the exact use of the term has changed over time,' and it did not always mean what we mean by it now. The wordIQ definition expands on this under the heading 'Use in psychiatry.'

> In his original attempt at classifying different forms of mental illness, Emil Kraepelin used the term *pure paranoia* to describe a condition where a delusion was present, but without any apparent deterioration in

intellectual abilities and without any of the other features of dementia praecox, the condition that was later to be renamed schizophrenia.

In the original Greek, παράνοια (paranoia) means self-referential, and it is this meaning which was adopted by Kraepelin. Notably, in this definition the belief does not have to be persecutory to be classified as paranoid, so any number of delusional beliefs which are centred around the self can be classified as paranoia. For example, a person who has the sole delusional belief that they are an important religious figure (such as Jesus or the Dalai Lama) would be classified by Kraepelin as having 'pure paranoia'.

Although the diagnosis of pure paranoia is no longer used (having been superceded by the diagnosis of delusional disorder) the use of the term to signify the presence of delusions in general, rather than persecutory delusions specifically, lives on in the classification of paranoid schizophrenia, which denotes a form of schizophrenia where delusions are prominent.

Paranoia was not always the fear of being followed, in other words, even if that is the fear I experienced leading up to and following each of my breaks. And when I say fear, I mean pure soul-draining fear, the kind that goes on without stopping. That is probably the worst thing about paranoia: it is unbelievably draining. Paranoia goes on for hours, for days, long past the need to eat and drink, long past the need to sleep, and for all that time you are drenched in fear, on edge, incapable of relaxing. Paranoia is exhausting.

Paranoia is the symptom I suffered most from, at first. During the second break, things changed, but during the first break and for the first part of the second break, paranoia was the thing that afflicted me. I remember one night, during the first break, when I drove around, believing people were following me. As I drove desperately around in the rain, I wrote their license plates numbers down on my arms. I believed that if I were killed, the police would be able to track those numbers. My mother could still see the writing when she came to see me in the hospital. And during my second break the magnitude of the conspiracy I believed in had become monumental; from a few individuals during the first break it had expanded to include whole government agencies during the second.

My shoes would be the last thing they saw when I went over the railing.

7.

Delusions. Again, from wordIQ.com:

> In the unrestricted use of the term, common para-
> noid delusions can include the belief that the person
> is being followed, poisoned or loved at a distance
> (often by a media figure or important person, a delu-
> sion known as erotomania or de Clerambault syn-
> drome).

> Other common paranoid delusions include the belief
> that the person has an imaginary disease or parasitic
> infection (delusional parasitosis); that the person is on
> a special quest or has been chosen by God; that the
> person has had thoughts inserted or removed from
> conscious thought; or that the person's actions are
> being controlled by an external force.

It was during my second break that my delusions really
took off.

During my first break, my primary delusion was that
I was being followed, that someone was trying to

hurt me. My delusions did not progress any further than that, probably because — due to my mother's cleverness — I ended up in the hospital so quickly.

During my second break, however, there was a period of weeks in which no one knew what was going on, largely because I actively concealed it. I was able to do this because, as Emil Kraepelin noted, though 'a delusion was present,' it was 'without any apparent deterioration in intellectual abilities,' (in other words, I was as smart as ever, if crazy) and it was the nature of my delusions — since I was dealing with a secret, shadowy conspiracy — that I had to keep quiet about it. *They*, after all, were watching.

Just who I believed *they* to be bears some examination, a quick overview.

They, I believed, was some part of the government, some secret agency connected to Homeland Security, that was out to preserve the contents of the book I had which detailed the fire department's role in 9/11, for which I had first worked as the designer, and then, in agreement with its author, was acting as agent, trying to get it published.

That was my first delusion.

They were pretty much everywhere, I believed, but so were the other *they*, the opposite forces, who wanted to keep the book from ever being seen, and who as part of that goal might wish me harm.

It wasn't a simple picture. I was being threatened, or I was being protected; I was working with someone, or I was working against someone; I had the truth about something, something that people wanted known or didn't want known. All that was clear to me, at that point, was that both sides were working in secrecy — I wasn't supposed to talk about it.

I kept it all to myself.

Because both sides were all around me, I began to watch the people I saw in the street, who I ran into in bars, who passed by me in the halls of my apartment building, wherever I was. I began to realize there was a code they communicated with, a series of gestures and looks that meant different things.

If you made a gesture that was like brushing dust from the arm of your coat, that meant *drop the subject*.

If you scratched the top of your head and looked puzzled, that meant *listen carefully*.

If you stroked your chin and looked thoughtful, that meant *think about this*.

I realized that people around me were making these gestures all the time. I saw my neighbor, who was a friend of mine (we often had dinner together), making these gestures. I noticed my other friend, Alisha, making them.

My friend Alisha was the one friend who saw a lot of me during this time. We met almost every day, or went out, and I frequently slept at her apartment. It was a good, platonic relationship.

It was Alisha, when things got bad enough, who suggested going to the hospital.

But not yet.

I noticed also that the people around me, the ones who made gestures, were all moving according to certain patterns. They had a way, out on the street, of telling you where to go. I spent many hours studying these patterns and trying to intuit what they meant.

Looking to the side meant *go that way*.

Walking quickly with your head down meant *keep going*

HEARING VOICES

I began to watch all around me all the time, trying to read these signals, and soon I noticed that there was a system in traffic for it too.

Revving your engine meant get moving.

Backing into a spot meant park it.

I gradually realized that nearly everything around me carried some kind of signal.

Get connected said one advertisement. *I can hear you now* said a billboard.

There was a moment when I finally had another kind of break, a moment when another delusion took over. I became convinced that most of society, in one way or another, was involved. There were signs everywhere — signs in the stores, telling you what to buy, signs on the Internet, signs on the streets. And the more I looked around, the more evidence I saw that not only were most people dealing with this system but actively promoting it.

I spent days, wandering the streets, following signs.

And then I realized that people could read your thoughts.

I realized this one morning after Alisha got up. I had spent the night at her house, working feverishly on the book — it still needed some editing — and I had stayed up the entire night. When she got up, she wandered into the living room, where I was working on the same computer I am working on now.

Alisha was the closest thing to family for me. She was the person I hung out with, and she was increasingly the person I depended on to guide me through this strange world I was just discovering. Alisha, it seemed to me, already knew about all these things.

Alisha, in other words, was one of *they* — the *they* who were my friends, the *they* I could count on.

It came to me in a flash, as I was talking to Alisha, that she could read my thoughts. I can no longer explain just how this happened — we were simply talking, trying to decide something so mundane as where to go for breakfast — but it happened instantaneously.

'People may insist, for example, that their thoughts are being broadcast or interfered with,' says the ICD-10.

After that, whatever rest I got was a matter of collapsing from exhaustion.

8.

The logic of delusions.

One simple form of a delusion is the conviction that random events going on around the person all relate in direct way to him or her. If you are walking down the street and a man on the opposite sidewalk coughs, you don't think anything of it and may not even consciously hear the cough. The person with schizophrenia, however, not only hears the cough but may immediately decide it must be a signal of some kind, perhaps directed to someone else down the street to warn him that the person is coming. The schizophrenia sufferer knows this is true with a certainty that few people experience. If you are walking with such a person and try to reason him/her past these delusions, your efforts will probably be futile. Even if you cross the street, and in the presence of the same person question the man about his cough, the individual will probably just decide that you are part of the plot. Reasoning with people about their delusions is like trying to bail out the ocean with a bucket. If, shortly after the cough incident, a helicopter flies overhead, the delusion may enlarge.

Obviously the helicopter is watching the person, which further confirms suspicions about the cough. And if in addition to these happenings, the person arrives at the bus stop just too late to catch the bus, the delusional system is confirmed yet again; obviously the person who coughed or the helicopter radioed the bus driver to leave. It all fits together into a logical, coherent whole.

This passage from *Surviving Schizophrenia*, by E. Fuller Torrey, M.D., describes better than anything else I have read the constant search for meaning that was such a driving force in my obsessive delusions. It was not just that people walked by me; it was that they were giving me signals, and each signal led to the next and that to the next and that to the next. As the schizophrenic Richard McLean put it so aptly in describing his own experience, 'I am forever on the verge of finding the secrets of the universe, yet they never manifest.'

*

There was a time, during my second break, when I started out walking, following the signs, and I did not make it home for three days.

What happened was that I had lost my car. Just how I had lost my car is another story unto itself.

Following the signals — at this point I believed they were everywhere — I went to the grocery store one evening and began to buy things. I had no idea what I was there for; I was just following the signals around me. The signals, I believed, were directing me to buy a number of things for a party — a couple of plastic tablecloths, a big jug for mixing juice or lemonade in, a big box of fireworks — and I realized that the intention, for whatever reason, was for me to have an outdoors party, probably a party for my daughter on the fourth of July. (It did not seem to matter, where the signals were concerned, if their purpose was exotic or mundane; the truth is that I could never quite figure out what they were intended for at all, whether I was being led slowly to some secret place or if the whole point of the signals was simply for me to learn them, for some future use.)

I purchased the items and took them out to my car, where — in traffic — the signals once again took over. This time I was led out to the freeway.

Signals on the road included *take the next turn, follow me, speed up* and *slow down*.

We followed the freeway for only a few hundred yards before we turned off. I was following a set of three cars that were racing along, following the signals for *follow me* and *take the next turn*. It was a turnoff that led, from the roads connected to it, into the hills that separate Portland from its suburb, Beaverton, a large city unto itself. The hills themselves have been built up significantly, but there are still large sections that consist of wooded areas. It was as we were going through one of these wooded sections that my car died. My car had never died before; I interpreted this to mean that this too was deliberate. There must have been some sort of device, I believed, that had caused the car to fail just there. It's true that I had been running out of gas, but it was obvious that I had been led here for a reason.

At this point I had come to believe that there was a system of sounds too, that there were certain sounds that meant *come this way*. A dog's barking, for instance, or the song of a bird. Just how a secret agency had come to control the sounds of birds and dogs was something I could not explain. It simply was.

I followed the sounds of a bird up the hill. When the sounds grew faint, I looked around me. There was a driveway leading to the right, a driveway lined with a series of lights, like a runway. I followed it. So far the system was working.

After a hundred yards or so, the gravel driveway led up to what appeared to be a relatively new house, nestled away in its own bit of woods. There was a Volvo station wagon of recent make in the driveway. From the back of the house, I heard a dog barking. I walked up to the door. Sitting on the doormat was a stick with a kind of cup on the end of it for hurling balls, hurling them as you would for dogs.

The appearance of this dog toy is something that merits comment, for the fact is that I had come to believe I was being trained, and the signals around me bore testimony to this fact; many of the people I saw in my neighborhood, and whom I watched, were leading dogs, which struck me even then as an unsubtle use of examples. I would watch them out the windows of my apartment, leading their dogs back and forth.

The pathway leading up to this doormat, to this stick, was a clear example then that the training was working.

From inside the house, I heard a woman calling 'here, boy!' and then 'good boy!' The words sounded recorded — as though there were tapes set to respond to the correct signal, such as someone approaching the house.

Just why I had been led to this house, I had no idea, but clearly I was meant to be here. Perhaps this person was meant to be my 'handler' — another coincidence in terminology between the secret society and animals. 'Here, boy,' and 'good boy' were meant for me.

I pushed the doorbell.

The woman who answered the door was a normal-looking woman in her mid-fifties, well-mannered and with a certain air of middle-class prosperity about her — clearly, a woman content in her circumstances. She asked how she could help me.

Not knowing how to work out a code for these things — the idea of coming right out and asking 'Are you my handler?' being out of the question — I explained to her what had happened: that the car had died, that I might need to use her phone. She offered, instead to give me a ride home.

It was while she was upstairs, briefly, that I saw a letter on her table that was signed by someone from a congressional office. I did not see what the letter said, but the fact that it was lying out in plain view seemed to me evidence that I was dealing with some government conspiracy.

While we were driving, before she dropped me off at home, I asked what she did.

'I'm a psychologist,' she said, and when I asked what kind, she said, 'Behavioral.'

My behavior was being re-oriented.

9.

I did not pick up my car immediately because I had forgotten that I had triple A. I also did not pick up my car immediately because I turned down Alisha's offer to go find it. The problem, I thought, was that I was out of gas, and that was something we could deal with in the morning.

That I had earlier thought it was something *they*'d done to the car did not even factor into my thinking.

Clearly, I had begun to have *disorganised thoughts*.

In fact, it was not until a couple of weeks later that I found out my car had actually been towed within a couple hours of its dying. It just never occurred to me to contact the authorities and ask about it, just as it never occurred to me that I had triple A.

*

I began looking for my car the next evening, after somehow — trying to understand the signals, looking for ambiguous meaning in everything — making it through a dinner with my other friend, my next-door neighbor. As unlikely as it seems, it appears that somehow, during all of this, I was not only pretending to be normal but actually succeeding. My mother says that the biggest outward change was in how polite I was. 'You were so incredibly polite to *everyone*,' she says. 'You called everyone *ma'am* and *sir*.' The truth is that the entire time I was listening carefully to everyone, trying to decode what *they* 'really' meant. It was part of my training, I thought, to pick up signals from everything, most especially conversations.

At the end of our meal, my friend dropped me off where I asked her to, on a street at the base of the Western Slope of Portland.

For the following three days, I did not stop moving. I did not stop to rest. I did not stop to eat, I did not stop to drink any coffee, and I ran out of cigarettes. My cell phone died when it ran out of charge. During the course of those three days, I wandered all the way between Beaverton and Portland more than once, following signals. At one point I spent several hours going back and forth in a development, in what I believed to be a 'fake' neighborhood, there explicitly for the purposes of training.

HEARING VOICES

At the end of the third day I was walking up the hill to Portland, coming back from Beaverton, when I began to walk along a road where you could look down over the entire city. Many houses of newer construction had been built along this ridge.

At this point I had reached a kind of high from not eating or stopping. I felt exhilarated, ready to keep going all the way home, where I planned to rest. As I was walking I passed a small roadhouse, one that looked like it had been there before the neighborhood had grown up around it. I knocked on the door, just as they were closing, and bummed a cigarette from the bartender who said she was closing up. I went back outside and kept going, until I passed what looked like a statue of a giant joker's head, although it is hard to remember; there were no lights shining on it, and the road was dark. But that was what I thought I saw. There was something about that head, carved into its lines and into the expression on its face, that was creepy, unsettling. I remember it as leering.

Of course, my memories of this are very poor — I had been up for three days — but this is what I *remember* seeing, and that is probably what matters.

A few yards, or a few hundred yards — that is the quality of my memory — further down the road, I passed a driveway. I had passed many driveways along the way, and had sometimes stopped and looked for a moment — there were many quite beautiful houses — but something about this house was different. First of all, it was not an impressive mansion like many of the houses I had been passing a few minutes earlier. It was smaller than those, almost a shack, and it sat back from the road in a little hollow of its own, almost a mythic glade, like one of those houses in the woods that old stories tell about. It transfixed me. It was lit up by the lights on the porch and by a light attached to the garage, which was detached. The house sat there in its own little circle of light.

Sitting in the yard, just a few from the door, there was a fountain. As I recall, it was shaped like a chalice, a giant chalice — again, as though it were taken from some old story. There were sculptures all around it, similarly of a mythic quality, all of which seemed in their diversity to represent various religions. The figure I remember best is that of a great carved-wood sculpture of a bear, standing upright, like a totem.

I walked up to the front door and knocked. No one answered. The house itself was dark; it was only the yard that was lit up with little landscaping lights, the kind that stand free on the lawn and spread their little pools of light. I could see through the front-door glass, and inside it looked plainly furnished.

I drank from the fountain, whose water ran clear and cold. Then I stood back and looked around.

All the sculptures were clustered close to the house on one side, the side where the driveway led up to a garage. On the other side there was simply a row of lights, leading along the grass, into the darkness.

A row of lights was one of the signals. At the dog lady's house, it was what had led me up the driveway.

I followed the lights to the edge of the yard, where darkness took over. The edge seemed to slope down, into a ravine, and it seemed to me that this was where the lights were indicating I should go. I followed the slope down. Soon, the soil began to drop down under my feet, a steep descent that seemed to go down ten or fifteen or twenty feet. Covering the ground, and all around me, there were trees and saplings and ferns, some of them live, some of them dead. At the bottom of the ravine it was dark, so dark that you could put your hand in front of your face and not know it was there.

Up above, there was a light. It was attached to the side of a building some distance away through the trees, a big flickering light almost like a giant bug light when it flashes; an incandescent, flickering light. It was a light that made me think of god.

I am not sure if I hallucinated there, because after a while the fronds of the plants around me began to waver in the fog around me; it seemed to create a spectral movement like the movement of spirits. I thought I could see the trees moving. But all I really know that happened is that at some point I fell asleep, because when I woke, half buried in the mud at the bottom of the ravine, I was panicked and desperate to get out of there. I knew, in that instantaneous way that has become so familiar, that I might have died in there, in what I thought of as god's ravine. God, I thought, wanted to kill me, and he had led me into the ravine to do it. I could think of no other explanation for the quality of that light, for the statues and the fountain, for that leering joker's head.

10.

There is something about the delusions that makes you wonder if, after having read about them all, you will get them too.

For instance, there was a woman in the mental hospital at the same time I was, a woman who suffered from 'anxiety attacks.' The particular source of her anxiety, as she was willing to tell anyone, was the idea that the world would simply end. It was an anxiety, as she explained it, which made it sound as if the world would simply *poof!* and disappear. When I first heard it, it seemed to me a bizarre delusion. *How would it feel*, I wondered, *to think that the world was about to end?* I tried it on for size. After a while, this idea seemed no stranger to me than the idea that time runs in an infinite direction both before we are born and after we die — a truth if there is one, but one which gives me no distress. It does not bother me, living this short life between two infinities, knowing that I did not exist at one time and knowing that I will not exist again. It does not bother me, but I can see how it might. It is simply that I have never taken that turning off the road of what I can control, off the road of sanity.

But I can see how I might.

It is the same with all the different delusions, about which I know a lot more than I once did.

There is the delusion that you are an important person, like Napoleon.

There is the delusion that god has chosen you for something, or that you are an important religious person like Jesus or Joan of Arc.

There is the delusion that someone is in love with you.

There is the delusion that people you know and love are imposters — fakes who replaced the real persons.

There is something about the delusions that is intrinsically — for those of us who don't have them — voyeuristic. Just as I imagine there has to be something voyeuristic in reading all these stories of mine (and so reliving them), so there is something voyeuristic about contemplating what it would be like to suffer from any particular delusion. What would it be like, one wonders, to feel as though I had a mission from god? What would it be like to feel as though I am the center of everything?

(I wonder these things just as, in a way, I imagine you wondering what it is like to feel persecuted, to feel that there is a conspiracy that controls society.)

The delusion that fascinates me most is the delusion called *delusional parasitosis*, the belief that you are infested with parasites. The very word, *parasitosis*, causes me to imagine strange bug-like creatures very much like the creature which the character played by Keanu Reeves in *The Matrix* has inserted through his belly button by 'the agents.' It is a creature that almost resembles a crayfish, with long antennae, that wriggles and squirms its way inside him. This is what I picture when I think of *parasitosis*, and I wonder, considering all the other delusions I have been susceptible to, if this might not be something that attacks me also. I wonder if simply knowing about that idea might cause me to ponder it a little too long, to develop it. But it never happens; I am simply not susceptible, it would seem, to that delusion. In fact, the knowledge that we have parasites — that certain bacteria live inside our bodies, or that microscopic crab-like creatures infest our eyelashes — bothers me not in the least.

Nevertheless, I feel relieved when I feel an itch on my skin and then, a few minutes later, notice the mosquito that has been pestering me. It is a relief to know that I am not, actually, hallucinating the effects of that delusion.

The delusion to which I am susceptible, I fear, is the delusion that thoughts are inserted or removed from one's head. I am afraid of this because of the nature of my own delusion of 'broadcasting' thoughts: that my thoughts can be read by other people. It seems too closely related to my own delusions, which makes me feel susceptible. After all, where do thoughts come from? In my experience, they simply pop into my head on their own, and disappear when they feel like it. They just sort of bubble up, as it were. Certainly I cannot say I am in control of the direction of my conscious thought; it is simply something I surf along, riding each wave as it finds me. For all I know, someone could be inserting my thoughts or taking them away.

So far I haven't taken that turning. But I can see how I might.

11.

It was when hallucinations got involved that things got really crazy.

'They may report hearing voices of varied kinds,' says the ICD-10.

> Voices may be heard that are not merely disparaging or condemnatory but that talk of killing the patient or discuss this behavior between themselves.

Fortunately, my own voices never quite got to the point of discussing 'this behavior between themselves,' although they came about as close to it as you can imagine. There were dozens of voices, and for a period of several weeks — until I got on the right medication, or until they simply stopped (it is impossible for me to know which) — they would not leave me alone, not for a minute, no matter how I begged. My head buzzed with their conversation from morning til night.

'An observer can't tell,' wrote Susanna Kaysen in her memoir *Girl, Interrupted*, 'if a person is silent and still because inner life has stalled or because inner life is transfixingly busy.'

In my case it was transfixingly busy.

*

I have always been fascinated by the word 'legion' in the Bible, and though I have never really known what it meant — I never took the time to look it up — I have always imagined it to mean that there is a horde of something, a horde of something evil.

It is hard to imagine a better description of what it was like to hear voices.

I remember an instance at one point, during my late twenties or early thirties, when I wondered what it would be like to hear voices. At that time I was slightly acquainted with a schizophrenic named Mike, who told me that he had Jesus in his head. That was his hallucination. Jesus talked to him, apparently. I remember wondering at the time what it would be like to have Jesus talking in my head.

What would it be like, I wondered, *to be schizophrenic for a day?*

HEARING VOICES

It turned out to be more terrifying than I ever imagined.

But I am getting ahead of myself. I haven't yet explained how the voices started.

One way of looking at it is to say that the voices started one morning in August of 2005. That is when they actually started — when I first heard them *talking*. But there is another way of looking at it, which is to say that they started when I began to *expect* them. There was actually a logic to this. You see, if people were reading my thoughts — that is, if they could *hear* me thinking — then it made sense to me that they would be able to *talk* to me too. The problem with me, I thought, was that I couldn't hear well enough. There was something wrong with my brain, something that kept me from being able to hear people's thoughts too. After all, it seemed to me, it was clear they were trying to get through to me.

I suffered with this thought for a period of weeks.

It is important to mention that during this time I moved back to the east coast. From the middle of June, my work was disrupted — as I began to follow the signs and to look for my car, a period of three or four weeks — and it became clear that I would not have my next month's rent. It is actually the one area in which I was 'in touch with reality.' It had also become clear to my mother by now, from the phone conversations that we had from time to time, that something was wrong again. I asked her to come get me — after wandering three days on foot, following signs, there was no way I could picture getting all the way across the country — and she agreed. Near the end of July, she took the train from New Hampshire to Oregon, where she helped me to pack up my apartment and then to drive my car back to New Hampshire. This was an experience for her. For five long days we drove across the country, while I, during the whole time, listened carefully to everything she said and often sat facing her, studying her every motion. She says that she was afraid to move after a while — that the way I would turn to face her, at her every move, was unsettling.

All during the drive, all I could do was sit and listen. At the time I was experiencing terrible delusions. At this time, as I have mentioned, I was convinced that more or less the whole country was tied into the conspiracy. As we drove across the country, I read the road signs and sides of trucks for their hidden meaning. Trucking companies, for instance, were always named something patriotic; there were Mayflower trucks, or American Trucking, for instance. Trucks always seemed to be decorated with red-white-and-blue; half of them had an American flag painted somewhere on the body. This seemed to me another one of the basic messages I was meant to understand — that this whole great conspiracy was one of great patriotism. It was not too much to say that the whole country was involved. Somehow I had missed this as I was growing up and going through life, but the time had come for me to learn.

At this time I had been psychotic about a month. I was worn down physically, from all the walking and from not eating. I was skinny as a rail. I ate Big Macs while we were on the road and I listened intently to whatever my mother said. My mother was my new *they*, I thought — the one who would help me clue into everything.

After a while, I was not able to walk through public places. This is because I had begun to feel intensely self-conscious, especially of my sexual organs. During my last week in Oregon, I could not seem to *not* feel them. I could not focus on another person without being aware of their genitalia under their clothes. It made walking through any public situation intensely embarrassing, and this continued while we were on the road. All I told my mother is that I didn't want to go into any of the restaurants we stopped at. It was only when I desperately needed the bathroom that I would enter any public space.

My mother, for her part, didn't know what to make of what was happening.

When we were driving through the Green Mountains of Vermont, within a couple hours of home, I began to feel a sort of pain in the side of my head. It was a sort of pain I was to become familiar with. What it meant was that people were near me, and I could tell from the side of my head that the pain was on where the people were located. During that drive through the mountains, I could feel the pain in the back of my head, from the people in back of us. (It continued when we were at home as well. In the daytime, when people were at work, the pain was minimal, if it existed at all, but as soon as people began to drive along the highway a few hundred yards from the house or once they came home from work to the houses surrounding our house, the pain would immediately start, a kind of burning pain that literally tracked the location of the people around me. Sometimes the pain was so intense that I literally tried to flee from one side of the house to the other, in hopes of making it less.)

I thought of this pain I would feel as 'stinging.' People were stinging me, sort of like bees, when they passed by.

HEARING VOICES

I began to notice other things about people as well, things that reminded me of bees. There was the way that they clustered, it seemed to me, wherever I would go. They simply moved as though they were in a hive — you could see this in any store you went into. All you had to do was go downtown — there they all were, moving around in their hive.

I had been back at my mother's for two weeks when I began to hear voices. It was a weekday and my mother was at work, but it had the feel of a Saturday, a summer Saturday. I was smoking a cigarette, dressed only in my shorts and a tee shirt, when suddenly in my head — in my own thoughts — a voice said, 'Are.'

Then, 'You.'

Then, 'Going.'

Then, 'To.'

Then, 'Be.'

Then, 'A.'

Then, 'Prick.'

Then, 'About.'

Then, 'This.'

It took me a minute to realize that it was a question, because each of the words was so individually punctuated, so nearly militaristically enunciated, that they came through one at a time. And then it asked again.

'Are. You. Going. To. Be. A. Prick. About. This.'

And then it asked again.

I remember the shock I felt that it had finally happened — not surprise that it happened, but that it finally had. Someone was clearly speaking to me *in my own head*.

My first reaction was panic. It is not every day, after all — and in my case it was thirty-six years — that a voice begins to speak to you internally.

My second reaction was to get to the hospital.

'Tell them you're feeling anxiety,' was the thought that came to me once again. All that mattered was going somewhere they could help me.

As it turned out, they could not help me very much.

12.

During my second break, I was in the hospital twice: once after the voices first started, and then again several weeks later. During the time between my two hospitalizations, the voices grew worse, never better. They began suddenly, and once they really got going they never stopped. That was the worst thing about them — that I could never get a break from them. They did not murmur in the background; there came a time when they demanded my attention every minute, almost every second. They wore down my endurance, day after day after day, week after week. At first medication did nothing to halt them.

If there were one thing that might have made the experience more bearable, it would have been if someone had actually given me some sort of prognosis or had told me something about the cause of the voices. But explanations were not forthcoming. If there was one thing I found, in fact, it was that doctors were, almost by their very nature, singularly uninformative. There was not a single one of them — either in the hospital I first went to, or in the New Hampshire state hospital where I later ended up — who dealt with the fact that I was hearing voices with anything more than a simple, flat acknowledgment. Each of them asked 'And I understand you are hearing some voices?' as though this were something so entirely normal that it hardly merited comment. Not one of them volunteered any information about what I was going through or made so much as an inquiry into the nature of what the voices were saying — a key piece of information, it seemed to me at the time, if ever there was one. The fact that I was no longer in control of my own thought process was treated in conversation as though it were no more significant than if I had a cold. Even the private doctor I eventually went to told me only that voices were considered 'non-diagnostic,' meaning that you could not base a diagnosis on them. This was puzzling until he explained that 'in the old days' it was enough simply to be hearing voices to be diagnosed a schizophrenic, meaning there were now enough different diagnoses to which hearing voices applied that it could no longer be used for diagnosis — thus 'non-diagnostic.' The one real piece of information I got was when I asked how common they were. The doctor I spoke to indicated that people hear voices all the time, much more than you'd think; it was about as common as diabetes, and 'most of the time it's of no consequence,' he said. Regarding the onset of voices, he said they simply came on — that 'one week you're fine, the next you're in the hospital.' That I was trying to home in on what exactly these voices were, what caused them, and — most important of all — how you could get rid of them was something he seemed to miss. The sum total of his wisdom seemed to be that 'It's easier to get than to get rid of.' This was not encouraging.

*

It was only later, however, that I began to seek real answers to what was going on. At first, I still believed they were supposed to be secret — part of the conspiracy, after all — and I did my best not to discuss them. It was only out of panic that I mentioned them to the people at the hospital the first time I was admitted. After that I kept my mouth shut.

And the voices, for that first week, were not terribly strong. On the hospital ward I was admitted to, where there were about a half dozen other patients and a staff of nurses and a doctor, I was able to listen to people and to carry myself as though things were normal. Most of the group meetings — times when people would check in and talk about what was going on for them, or when we would be asked to watch a video and discuss it afterwards — were mostly irrelevant for me; I sat through them quietly and was glad when they were over. The rest of the time I did my best to sit alone in my room; never mind that isolation is one of the key indicators that something is wrong.

Over the couple of weeks before I was admitted, religion had become a kind of obsession for me. It started with the house on the hill and continued with whatever I was doing. Anything I read, it seemed to me, was full of significance; books seemed to be describing something beyond their nominal topics, although I was never sure what that was. 'I am forever on the verge of finding the secrets of the universe, yet they never manifest,' as Richard McLean put it. One night I had sat out on the porch during a rainstorm, and I thought the flashes of lightning and booms of thunder were connected somehow to my thought process; I thought they were god's way of answering my thoughts.

While I was in the hospital, one of the people who came in to see us was a social worker and minister named John, who talked to us about whatever was on our minds and about things like meditation. One day he brought in a poem by Rilke, 'The Man Watching.' ('The man watching' from *Selected Poems of Rainer Maria Rilke, A Translation from the German and Commentary* by

HEARING VOICES

I can tell by the way the trees beat, after
so many dull days, on my worried windowpanes
that a storm is coming,
and I hear the far-off fields say things
I can't bear without a friend,
I can't love without a sister.

The storm, the shifter of shapes, drives on
across the woods and across time,
and the world looks as if it had no age:
the landscape, like a line in the psalm book,
is seriousness and weight and eternity.

What we choose to fight is so tiny!
What fights with us is so great!
If only we would let ourselves be dominated
as things do by some immense storm,
we would become strong too, and not need names.

When we win it's with small things,
and the triumph itself makes us small.
What is extraordinary and eternal
does not want to be bent by us.

I mean the Angel who appeared
to the wrestlers of the Old Testament:
when the wrestlers' sinews
grew long like metal strings,
he felt them under his fingers
like chords of deep music.

Whoever was beaten by this Angel
(who often simply declined the fight)
went away proud and strengthened
and great from that harsh hand,
that kneaded him as if to change his shape.
Winning does not tempt that man.
This is how he grows: by being defeated,
decisively, by constantly greater beings.

Here at last was something that frankly addressed the
subject of god, that came out and told me something
spiritual was going on. 'This is how he grows: by being
defeated, decisively, by constantly greater beings.' I
took this to mean that everything I was going through
had a purpose, that I was meant to hear voices, and all
my efforts that first week went toward trying to hear
them better.

John was an almost unbelievably kind man, and he was
probably a wonderful counselor for people dealing

with depression or perhaps with grief over the loss of a loved one, but I am not sure he was such a good counselor for someone dealing with paranoid delusions. It is not too much to say that he contributed a lot to mine.

13.

I had been staying with my mother, but while I was in the hospital she went out and found an apartment for me, rented it, and moved my things in. She knew I wanted my privacy and renting an apartment for me was the kindest thing she could do. She did not realize what horrible shape I was in or what even worse shape I was soon to be in; that there was no way, in fact, that I would go out and get a job to pay for this apartment that she had found. It was when I was alone that the voices really took over.

I had been in the hospital for only eight days. The normal stay was ten days, but I had insisted, after initially admitting that I was hearing voices, that I was fine, there was nothing wrong, and after eight days of this they capitulated and released me. I was compliant about taking any medication they chose to give me — as I was throughout my illness — but clearly it did not have any effect.

In fact I had been doing my best to tune in to what the voices were saying the entire time.

At first it was almost like I was listening to a radio with a lot of static. The voices were there, but they came through indistinctly most of the time. They would fade in and out. I would sit there, almost catatonic, and strain to hear them. And the few times I could hear them clearly they asked me to do something bizarre. They wanted me to masturbate 'with a beautiful woman in your head' and a finger up my ass.

This is how they brought you into focus, they said. The whole nervous system, from the prostate near the base of the spine and up the spine to your head, was like a radio, and this was how a man tuned in.

I did what they told me — several times. In the hospital, it is remarkable that someone did not walk into my room and catch me doing this, considering how often the staff checked in on us. I was not even bothering to go into the bathroom to do it.

Once I was out of the hospital and installed in my new apartment it was no longer necessary for me to do this, as the voices began to come through loud and clear. And this is when a new kind of Vortex took over.

14.

The sheer variety of the voices and what they talked about is almost impossible to capture, but there are highlights. And because almost all the voices belonged to people I knew (or knew of, in the case of political figures) and because of my own profound lack of insight into my illness (I did not believe I was ill at all, but simply coming to a new understanding of reality), I believed everything they told me.

I was fortunate in that there was only one truly malign voice, which is to say a voice that hated me. Many schizophrenics report voices that abuse them and tell them to hurt or even kill themselves, the so-called 'command hallucinations.' In my case most of the voices wanted to help me, if you wish to go so far as to call the bizarre range of information they gave me 'help.'

*

One reason that has occurred to me that explains why the doctors and nurses in the psych wards where I stayed never bothered to ask what the voices were talking about is that they were powerless to do anything about it: that is, there was nothing they could do even if they wanted to. The other reason that occurs to me is that what the voices are talking about can change incessantly; that trying to keep up with it all is like trying to drink from a fire hose.

Of what I can remember, the primary topic initially was the subject of hearing and communicating with other people's thoughts. Yes, *they* could hear me, and yes, *they* could talk to me and I could talk back to *them*. It was referred to as being 'psychic,' rather obviously, and it had existed throughout human history. A few people had always been able to read other people's thoughts and to communicate with each other, although this had been rare. In the old days they had mostly gone under the rubric of 'mystic,' although some of them had been leaders who used these powers to gain control of other people — discovering others' political plans, ferreting out war strategies, and so on.

This had begun to change in the twentieth century, when a few of these psychics had discovered that it was possible to turn a normal person into a psychic, to 'pop their cork.' This discovery had been made in the United States, and from the 1970s on more and more people were made into psychics. And the United

States, being what they are, had taken advantage of this. It was not long before the government was infiltrated with psychics who decided to use these powers to help control the world. A group of psychic CIA agents, if you think about it, is no joke; psychics contributed to our victory in the Cold War, psychics hunted down criminals and terrorists, psychics worked in industry to discover other nations' industrial secrets. Eventually, as the conversions of normal people — called 'assholes' for some reason, which is why even friendly voices referred to me constantly as 'asshole' — gained pace through the eighties and nineties, the whole country verged on being psychic. Most people had their corks popped in their teenage years, although the conversion of older people continued. Teenagers and young people had even developed a kind of sadistic game of popping unsuspecting people's corks and then leaving them to scream in terror at what was happening to their minds. Obviously, no detail was too small for my voices to deal with.

What screwed up the American hegemony was the porosity of societies. Some people who came to this country — for college, for work or vacation — had their corks popped, figured out what it was all about and went back to their own countries. Though their numbers overall were still small, psychics had begun to take over societies in Europe and Russia and to a lesser extent in other countries. America would not be the only psychic society for long.

What made me unusual was that no one had come along and popped my cork at the advanced age of thirty-five.

Psychics had varying degrees of power and of control over themselves. One example would be the sound of their voice. Most psychics talked to you in your thoughts quietly and individually, almost like a private phone call between two people, but some people had no control over their thoughts and broadcast to everyone within range of their thoughts, setting up a constant background noise to everyone around them. A weak psychic with this problem might be audible within a couple hundred yards, a powerful one for a couple miles. Normal people — assholes — could not hear this, but other psychics could, and at night, trying to sleep, they might have a powerful but uncontrolled psychic blasting thoughts into their brains all night. A general rule was that the younger you were when your cork was popped the greater your control over your power.

This is where I had a problem. Apparently — according to what the voices said — I was an unusually powerful psychic. When my cork was popped — something that always created a kind of psychic explosion, an initial release of energy — psychics could hear it for the better part of a hundred miles. Immediately I began to hear from people all over the place both congratulating me on joining the community and telling me to shut up. I had no control yet, they said, and they could hear me for miles. I felt ashamed — and panicked — but could do nothing about it.

*

During the weeks leading up to having my cork popped — which would enable me to hear other people's thoughts even when they weren't talking to me, even normal people's, and to take control of other powers as well — much of the conversation revolved around something called Asshole of the Month.

In psychics' minds, I was told, there was a kind of visual area, much like a TV screen, through which they could see through other psychics' eyes. At any given time you might be watching through a friend's eyes or through the eyes of other people who broadcast 'shows,' these being people who ranged from celebrities to any man on the street. There was only one catch: you had to have one of these shows going in your mind all the time, regardless of who it belonged to. You might be watching someone having sex, for instance. You might be watching someone catch fish. No matter what, it had to be someone, and as a result the psychics had put together a kind of network that broadcast a number of shows that were available to anyone, including Asshole of the Month. On Asshole of the Month, the psychics picked one asshole — someone who hadn't had their cork popped yet — and broadcast what that person went through in the weeks just before, during, and after having their cork popped. In many ways it was a joke. An asshole was picked who had no idea what was going on and was essentially pranked by the organizers of the show. Sometimes the asshole was told that he had been chosen by god to save the world, for example; in whatever case, the asshole was led down the garden path and shown up for the asshole he was.

I was chosen for Asshole of the Month.

*

There was a voice — the voice of the author of the book I had been working on when all this started — who told me that I was someone special, that I had been chosen to be The One.

There were a certain number of people who were special. They were given special powers and were expected to serve people in special roles.

The One was a kind of military leader. He had appeared throughout history and led his people to supremacy. These days he was American. Previously people who had been The One were George Washington and Abraham Lincoln — people who had led our country through crises and come out successful.

I never was told who all the people who had been The One were, but most recently there had been General George Patton, who led armies through World War II. Patton had died in an accident, but not before he passed being The One on to a common sergeant named Albrecht Dürer — not, as one might suspect, the northern Renaissance painter, but a member of Patton's army. You did not have to be a leader in the army, but simply someone with the drive and qualifications to carry on as a leader. Dürer had served as The One through Korea and passed along the duty to another man in Vietnam — the man who had written the book I had been hired to design and sell.

As The One I would wield immense power.

There were some in the establishment who objected to a non-military person being The One. But the choice was that of The One, and he had chosen me.

There were other special people who were to be associated with me.

The Bearer of Light was to be my best friend, David. Bear in mind that "The Bearer of Light" in Latin is "Lucifer," although there was nothing in the discussion that suggested any malefic intent about being The Bearer of Light. He was the one who would advise me and help organize the armies of The One. The previous Bearer of Light was Donald Rumsfeld, the Secretary of Defense.

There was La Conchita — the Conch — who was a sort of broadcaster of information. This was to be my sister.

It was important that we all work together as a team. That La Conchita was working with me was a new development, but whenever one of the special ones met each other it was a good thing.

When I was chosen as The One, I was introduced to a number of important people. There was John Kerry, the former Presidential candidate and Senator from Massachusetts. There was Condoleeza Rice, the Secretary of State. There was Donald Rumsfeld, the Secretary of Defense. And there was the President, George W. Bush. All of these people talked to me briefly and congratulated me on being The One.

I have no idea now if the voices really meant that I was The One or if they were just leading me down the garden path as they always did for the Asshole of the Month.

*

But this is not all the voices were up to. There was also the game show.

It is important to consider that none of the voices were consistent. At one time they might be talking to me about the nature of being psychic and a little while later about being The One. They switched constantly. And at some point the game show started.

One of the rewards of being Asshole of the Month was that you had a chance at winning the lottery. Unless, of course, the other players in the game show outwitted you.

I cannot with clarity recall exactly how the game show worked, nor can I recall what the purpose of the game show was; only that it involved twelve people, all of whom were close to me: my best friend David; David's wife Sabrina; my mother; Tanya, the mother of my daughter; Tanya's mother Julie; Tanya's sister Debbie; Debbie's husband Bruce; my former therapist Darron; my friend Alisha; and a shifting cast of others whom I had known. There was some strange goal of putting together an alliance that would enable the winner to win a lottery of the strangely exact amount of fifty-seven million dollars. You could work with me, or you could put together an alliance with the other players to claim the lottery for yourself.

*

As I mentioned earlier, the younger you were when you had your cork popped the greater was your control over your powers. People with control could prevent others from reading their thoughts, could communicate with others successfully, and had other powers as well. One of these groups of powers was the ability to attack others and to defend yourself from attack.

Because I was the Asshole of the Month I attracted some unwelcome attention. Some of this was from disturbed individuals, who tried to gain control of my mind or hurt me. It was possible to direct your concentration in such a way that you could cause a kind of flash of pain in another person's head much like the sting of a bee. It was a kind of burning pain that felt like a little explosion in your head. I had this done to me a number of times and — being the powerful psychic that I was — I did it in retaliation as well. It turned out I was quite good at it. At one point I had quite a battle with a known killer in prison — and just because you were in prison didn't mean you couldn't be quite a powerful psychic. On the contrary: prisoners had little to prevent them from spending all their time developing their skills.

Because a psychic without good control was open to all sorts of problems — broadcasting out of control, having their minds manipulated, being attacked — there were many psychics who helped them put up a kind of psychic armor. Having this armor, which was not really under their control but set up for them by others, was called being a 'robot.' Your defenses were automated, the strength of your broadcasting controlled. Some psychics were little more than prisoners of their armor. And because you had to give some of your psychic power to the ones who controlled their defenses, they were often reduced to being little more than power sources for others — what was called being a 'fuel dump.' They were looked down upon by the psychics who had learned to control their powers on their own.

This is where I had a problem. Since I was unusually powerful and since I had had no time to develop control over my own powers, I was besieged by groups of psychics who had gotten together for mutual defense and influence, groups that often organized by profession or other affiliation — the National Guard, the CIA, the police, for instance — who tried to force me into joining their group. I resisted them all. I did not want to be anyone's fuel dump. I did not want to be a robot. I wanted to learn to control my powers on my own.

These groups were relentless. They would not leave me alone, pestering me night and day, constantly talking to me. Finally I made contact with a powerful psychic — a kind of legend, they said — from the prison guards' union. Prison guards may sound like an odd choice, but they dealt with the most powerful inmates and mastered them, dealing with levels of thought control and psychic attacks dealt with by few others. All they wanted from me was a little bit of my power, he said; in return they would protect me, and no one wanted to mess with them.

I almost made a deal with them. But really what I wanted was to be left alone — for a few days, a few hours, or even a few minutes. But that was not to be.

15.

The pain is unrelenting, and what makes the condition intolerable is the foreknowledge that no remedy will come — not in a day, an hour, a month, or a minute. If there is mild relief, one knows that it is only temporary; more pain will follow. It is hopelessness even more than pain that crushes the soul. So the decision-making of daily life involves not, as in normal affairs, shifting from one annoying situation to another less annoying — or from discomfort to relative comfort, or from boredom to activity — but moving from pain to pain. One does not abandon, even briefly, one's bed of nails, but is attached to it wherever one goes. And this results in a striking experience — one which I have called, borrowing military terminology, the situation of the walking wounded. For in virtually any other serious sickness, a patient who felt similar devastation would be lying flat in bed, possibly sedated and hooked up to the tubes and wires of life-support systems, but at the very least in a posture of repose and in an isolated setting. His invalidism would be necessary, unquestioned and honorably attained. However, the sufferer from depression has no such option and therefore finds himself, like a walking casualty of war, thrust into the most intolerable social and family situations. There he must, despite the anguish devouring his brain, present a face approximating the one that is associated with ordinary events and companionship. He must try to utter small talk, and be responsive to questions, and knowingly nod and frown and, God help him, even smile. But it is a fierce trial attempting to speak a few simple words.

Except that this excerpt from William Styron's *Darkness Visible* is talking about the anguish of depression, it might describe the agony of constantly hearing voices. It was not the fact of hearing voices itself that was torture; that could have been dealt with. No, it was their unrelenting presence, their absolute and never-ending refusal to leave me alone.

Consider the fact that when taken into custody by police, strong men will break down after eighteen or twenty hours' questioning and confess to any crime they are accused of, regardless of their innocence. Human endurance will go only so far. Now consider that I had been plagued by voices that refused to stop talking to me for months, even when I wept and begged for a few minutes' respite. That I lasted as long as I did is a kind of testimony to the human spirit.

I felt my will break one night when I was sitting on my mother's porch. I had given up any pretence to wanting my own apartment and now spent every day at her house, sleeping over and spending as much time with her as possible. This did not mean I could effectively communicate with her; while I might attempt to make conversation, the voices continued to drone on, distracting my attention and causing me to lose the thread of any discussion we might have. The night my will was broken she was inside while the voices that had been badgering me all day continued their assault. They said that I had to choose: I would belong to this organization or another, and that I had to choose. But I refused; I did not want to give away my autonomy, to be under someone else's control. And then they attacked me in a way they never had before: I felt myself go rigid, unable to move, unable to speak, while inside I screamed to be let go. And when I felt my will break, knowing that I could no longer resist them, that after all the weeks of constant badgering I had nothing left with which to resist, I gave up all hope. I would never be free; the only thing left was to submit.

As William Styron also wrote,

> I had now reached that phase of the disorder where
> all sense of hope had vanished, along with the idea

of a futurity; my brain, in thrall to its outlaw hormones, had become less an organ of thought than an instrument registering, minute by minute, varying degrees of its own suffering.

The next morning I got up, heard the voices begin talking to me, and went into the kitchen and told my mother I needed her help killing myself.

16.

> He was friendly to the medical staff and they liked him,
> but since he did not believe there was anything wrong
> with him or that he should be confined in a mental
> hospital, he saw them, at least in part, as prison war-
> dens to be outwitted at every opportunity.

This passage from Patrick and Henry Cockburn's
Henry's Demons captures exactly the mindset I had
about sharing what was going on — the delusions, the
hallucinations — with the staff of whichever hospital
I was in. I was not hallucinating, so I believed, but having a spiritual experience, an awakening to what the
world was really like. The real world I had always
known was still there but there were new layers added
on to it, and much of my efforts during my psychosis
were efforts to understand these new dimensions of reality. It is not that a psychotic is necessarily devoid of
reason; it may simply be that the premise of their
thinking — their starting point — is wrong.

The understanding that you are sick and that what is
going on is a manifestation of that illness is called

'insight' by the psychiatric profession: 'insight' into the nature of your condition. A man with a broken arm does not lack insight into his condition, but schizoaffective illness and the schizophrenia and bipolar disorder of which mine was composed are all notorious for a lack of insight. That is, people who are sick frequently have no idea they are sick; they believe they are having a special experience, frequently spiritual. This is one of the things that lead in so many cases to a sick person's resisting or even refusing to take medication. In my own case, until I was properly medicated, I had no insight at all. I truly believed that what was going on was real, that it was secret knowledge not to be shared with other persons, and that sooner or later I would be enlightened about what was going on and would as a result be a more successful and happy person. The doctors I dealt with — and my mother, who slogged along through the drifts of my psychosis with the patience of a saint — had the additional hurdle of overcoming my resistance in every way they tried to help me. This did not make me any easier to deal with.

*

After I told my mother that I needed her help in killing myself she went into another room where I could not hear her and called the police. A few minutes later, sitting outside and smoking a cigarette, I saw the police pull up and knew that something was wrong. They approached. They talked to me for a few minutes — we understand you're having some problems, etc., etc. — then told me that I should put on my shoes and come with them. I refused to put on my shoes. Everything was fine, I said, I was not going anywhere. This was all a mistake. They told me I could put on my shoes or they would take me the way I was. Still I refused. And then they took me by the arms, stood me up, put me in handcuffs and took me away.

17.

Recently I watched the movie *Marwencol*. This story of a man who was brain-damaged after a brutal beating gave me much to relate to. After six months of florid, rampant psychosis your life is destroyed and you don't just come back where you left it — like him. Like him, I had to deliberately and consciously teach myself how to do things again — not so far as having to teach myself how to write again, as he did, but in everything that might be described as 'living.' I had to start small and work my way up. I had to learn how to watch TV — to follow the plots, to focus attention, etc. After that I taught myself how to read, to work up from cheap novels to books that one might call challenging. I had to learn to go down to a bar and have a conversation with people. I'm still socially challenged but I belong to a pool league and have a couple friends and that gives me some social interaction — one of the great problems people like me face is social isolation. Playing pool came back surprisingly easily. I had to force myself to listen to National Public Radio and become involved in the world again. One of the things that happened during my psychotic time was the devastation of hurricane Katrina in New Orleans. I cannot tell you how hard it was for me to comprehend what was happening: my mind was so inwardly focused that it took months for me to grasp. One thing that has never quite returned is my sense of language: that hard-won sense of every nuance and rhythm that used to guide my writing and my criticism of others which was a substantial part of my sense of self. All this -- and never mind that I had to slowly teach myself that no, no one was reading my mind, there was no government conspiracy against me, and the countless other delusional beliefs that had taken control of all my perceptions and actions. All in all it took a couple years to come back from a semi-catatonic and bullshit-crazy state to something that at least approximates normality, and praise god that I found a medication that did not have the bizarre and uncomfortable side effects that most of them have. It is true that I have gained weight — a lot of weight — but this seems a small price to pay for having my mind back. And so the movie *Marwencol* has been a bit of a trigger for memories of what happened and what it took to recover. Any glimpse of someone's recovery has no trace any longer of the vicarious weirdness-pleasure it had when I was normal but it does give me a little gratification in relating to it, and gratitude for the grace of god that some kind of recovery does exist.

Of course I still suffer symptoms. Generally, symptoms are referred to as being of two types: 'positive' and 'negative.' Positive symptoms include hallucinations and delusions, that is, symptoms that are positively there, traits that stand out from the normal. My positive symptoms have mostly abated. I still hear voices at times, but I am able to ignore them and they dissipate. The delusions — that I might win the lottery or that a secret society wanted to control me — have gone away. Negative symptoms are somewhat harder to understand. They might be described as deficits, that is, qualities that someone lacks. They include a lack of displayed emotion, an inexpressive expression, a lack of motivation, a lack of pleasure in what they're doing or feeling, a lack of a social instinct, a lack of speech or verbosity. I have all of these lacks. They make it hard for me to be part of a group; that is, I am noticeably less social, less expressive than the people around me. I am not motivated to do anything, be it exercise or work or time with others. I rarely feel pleasure, except from music, which strangely still gives me the pleasure I always had — and for this I am truly grateful. I am most comfortable in my own space or in that of a very few friends. My stimulation comes from reading — an isolated experience. People in public situations tend to shun me — not because I do anything to offend them but because I am different: quiet, inexpressive, solitary. I don't add much to most conversations, and I don't laugh at jokes that most often do not strike me as funny. I accept this. It is like suffering a low-grade depression all the time. Modern medications are effective in treating the positive symptoms but not so much for the negative symptoms. I am grateful for the relief I have from positive symptoms and accept the rather limited relief from the negative. I do have a few friends who appreciate who I am and whom I appreciate in turn. I feel that this is all I can ask. I'm functional; I have satisfaction from my life; I don't need to be perfect.

One last word. Most schizophrenics, I have noticed, believe that their hallucinations and attendant delusions are a spiritual experience that others — the normal — simply have not experienced. When I was going through these things this is what I too believed. There is a difference between myself and most other people with the same experience, however: namely that I was older at the time of onset of my hallucinations and delusions than most people are. I did not experience schizoaffective hallucinations and delusions until I was in my mid-thirties, much later than the usual onset of age twenty or thereabouts. This means that I was a fully developed human being — socially, spiritually, intellectually — as opposed to the growing-up period that most people in the same situation are going through. They do not have the same deeply ingrained sense of the world and who they are. I had a fully developed worldview, a fully developed sense of myself, and this means that when I recovered I had something to fall back on. That is, when I finally realized I was crazy, I had well-developed beliefs from my previous life that I was able to remember and gradually resurrect. This is not to say it was easy. But there was something to reclaim. When you are only twenty and suddenly you have hallucinations, your belief that this is purely a spiritual experience has no counter-claim to go against it. You believe that you are receiving special messages — nothing in your experience tells you that this is impossible — and you are at the age when many spiritual beliefs are being formed. And so many people, despite whatever recovery, despite whatever medications, continue to believe that the hallucinations and delusions are in some way a real reflection of the real world. Fortunately I am old enough to know how strange all these hallucinations and delusions are. I have a base, a clear sense of self that I was able to fall back on. This is the basis of my recovery. Most people I meet have no idea that there is anything wrong with me and I am able to pass as though there is nothing wrong: strange, perhaps, but not mentally ill. It is my secret and the secret of the few that I trust. I long for the day when it will no longer be necessary for it to be a secret, for the mentally ill to be accepted for what they are and what they can give — instead of the usual reactions of fear and misunder-standing — but there is no telling what the future will bring.

ABOUT THE AUTHOR

Eric Coates grew up in New Hampshire. He attended Bard College and lived in numerous cities, including New York, San Francisco and Portland, Oregon. *Hearing Voices* is his first book. His other books include *Cracking Up: A Memoir of Love, Drinking, Drugs, Poverty, Paranoia, and Other Afflictions on the Road to Madness* and *Smoking: An Intimate History.*

Made in the USA
Lexington, KY
08 December 2014